W9-BAU-707

Team Spirit

THE INDIANAPOLIS COLTS

BY

MARK STEWART

Content Consultant
Jason Aikens
Collections Curator
The Professional Football Hall of Fame

NORWOODHOUSE PRESS
CHICAGO, ILLINOIS

Norwood House Press
P.O. Box 316598
Chicago, Illinois 60631

For information regarding Norwood House Press, please visit our website at:
www.norwoodhousepress.com or call 866-565-2900.

All photos courtesy AP/Wide World Photos, Inc. except the following:
Topps Company Inc. (pages 18, 20, 21, 34, 35, 38, 39, 40, 43)
Bowman Gum Company (pages 30, 34); Exhibit Supply (page 36), TCMA (page 40)
Special thanks to Topps, Inc.

Editor: Mike Kennedy
Designer: Ron Jaffe
Project Management: Black Book Partners, LLC.

Special thanks to: Kathleen Baxter, Meredith Mason, and Laura Peabody.

Library of Congress Cataloging-in-Publication Data

Stewart, Mark.
    The Indianapolis Colts / by Mark Stewart ; with content consultant Jason
Aikens.
       p. cm. -- (Team spirit)
    Summary: "Presents the history, accomplishments and key personalities of
the Indianapolis Colts football team. Includes timelines,quotes,maps,
glossary and websites"--Provided by publisher.
    Includes bibliographical references and index.
    ISBN-13: 978-1-59953-005-5 (library edition : alk. paper)
    ISBN-10: 1-59953-005-8 (library edition : alk. paper) 1. Indianapolis
Colts (Football team)--History--Juvenile literature. 2. Baltimore Colts
(Football team)--History--Juvenile literature. I. Aikens, Jason. II. Title. III.
Series.
    GV956.I53S85 2006
    796.332'640977252--dc22
                                           2005029906

Manufactured in the United States of America.

COVER PHOTO: The Indianapolis Colts celebrate after a touchdown in a 2004 game.

Table of Contents

SPORTS WORDS & VOCABULARY WORDS: In this book, you will find many words that are new to you. You may also see familiar words used in new ways. The glossary on page 46 gives the meanings of football words, as well as "everyday" words that have special football meanings. These words appear in **bold type** throughout the book. The glossary on page 47 gives the meanings of vocabulary words that are not related to football. They appear in ***bold italic type*** throughout the book.

Meet the Colts

A football team needs a strong leader. When the game is going well, he keeps the other players focused. When nothing is going right, he keeps their spirits high. The Indianapolis Colts have always looked to their quarterbacks for this leadership. It is a *tradition* that stretches back more than 50 years.

The spirit of the Colts comes from more than their quarterbacks, however. The team has some of the most loyal and loving fans in football. They are loud and they are proud. They have cheered for the Colts through thick and thin, and they treat the players like family.

This book tells the story of the Colts. They have won glorious victories and suffered heartbreaking defeats. They have gotten the job done with glittering superstars, and tough, *tenacious* warriors. Some of the greatest heroes and most colorful characters in football have worn the blue and white of the Colts. That is just as true today as it was years ago. That is why the Colts are so proud of their past, and so excited about their future.

Peyton Manning calls a play. Like the quarterbacks who came before him, Manning became a team leader for the Colts.

Way Back When

The story of the Colts begins in the late 1940s, when football was just beginning to become the popular sport it is today. There were two leagues back then, the **National Football League (NFL)** and the **All-America Football Conference (AAFC).** In 1947, the AAFC moved one of its teams to Baltimore, Maryland. They were called the Colts.

Baltimore fans loved their new team. They did not win very often, but they passed the ball a lot, and their games were usually exciting. In 1950, after the AAFC went out of business, the Colts joined the NFL. After losing 11 times in 12 games, they went out of business, too.

In 1953, a Baltimore businessman named Carroll Rosenbloom brought a new NFL team to his city. He named the team the Colts. Baltimore fans were thrilled to have a second chance to watch professional football. More than 150,000 people bought tickets to their six home games in 1953.

Many of the Colts' players came from the Dallas Texans and Cleveland Browns. The Texans had been one of the worst teams in the NFL in 1952, and the Browns had been one of the best. These

Art Donovan hears the roar of the crowd in Baltimore before a game. He was the first member of the Colts to be voted into the Hall of Fame.

players included Art Donovan, Gino Marchetti, Don Shula, Buddy Young, Tom Keane, and Bert Rechichar. Over the next few years, the Colts added other good players, including Jim Parker, Alan Ameche, Lenny Moore, and Raymond Berry. The team's leader was Johnny Unitas, the best quarterback in the league.

In 1958, the Colts played the New York Giants for the **NFL Championship**. It was a thrilling game that was tied 17–17 after four quarters. The Colts won in **overtime**. It was the first time an NFL game had ended this way. Millions of television viewers watched the game, and were on the edge of their seats right to the very end. They became instant NFL fans.

The Colts won the NFL championship in 1959 and again in 1968. After their victory in 1968, they played the **American Football League (AFL)** champions, the New York Jets, in **Super Bowl** III. The Colts lost 16–7. Baltimore made it back to the Super Bowl two years later and played the Dallas Cowboys in Super Bowl V. The Colts won 16–13 on a **field goal** in the final seconds.

The Colts were very good during the 1970s, but they did not win another championship. The owner of the Colts, Robert Irsay, thought a new stadium would improve the team's luck. The State of Maryland did not want to spend the money, and Irsay did not want to pay for a new stadium himself. So in 1984, he packed up the team's equipment and moved the Colts to Indianapolis, Indiana.

The Colts nearly made it back to the Super Bowl several years later. On the last play of the 1995 **American Football Conference (AFC)** championship game, Jim Harbaugh's desperate pass into the end zone fell to the ground an inch from his receiver's fingertips. Though disappointed, the Colts and their fans vowed they would return to the Super Bowl one day.

LEFT: Johnny Unitas
RIGHT: Receiver Aaron Bailey tries to catch a tipped pass from Jim Harbaugh on the last play of the 1995 AFC championship game.

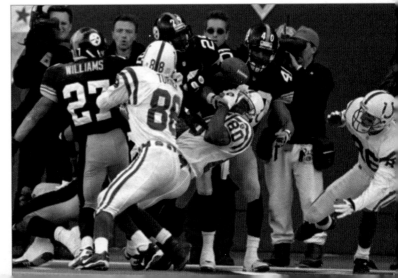

The Team Today

The Colts have become one of the most exciting teams in football. It all began in the late 1990s, when they **drafted** Marvin Harrison, Edgerrin James, and Peyton Manning.

Harrison, a wide receiver, was small for the NFL, but he always found a way to get open. James, a running back, had the perfect combination of power, speed, and tricky moves. Manning, a quarterback, began setting passing records in his first season. He seemed to break a new one every year after that.

The Colts built around these players and became a championship *contender*. They are fun to watch, but they are no fun to play. They find the weak spots in a defense and attack it until they reach the end zone. If a team can stop the Colts, they have really *accomplished* something.

Peyton Manning and Edgerrin James leave the field together after a victory by the Colts. These two stars helped the Colts become one of the best teams in the NFL.

Home Turf

The Colts play in the RCA Dome. The stadium stands 19 stories tall. Its roof is covered with ***Teflon-coated fiberglass***. Winters in Indianapolis are very cold and windy. The stadium's domed roof protects players and fans from bad weather. The Colts' home is located right in the heart of Indianapolis.

The stadium is very clean and ***spacious***. People who visit from others cities say that the fans have very good manners. Of course, when the Colts need a big play, it can get very noisy very fast. There have been times when the players could not hear one another in the **huddle**!

THE RCA DOME BY THE NUMBERS

- *There are 55,506 seats in the RCA Dome.*
- *The roof weighs 257 tons.*
- *The stadium opened in 1983.*
- *The RCA Dome was called the Hoosier Dome until 1994.*
- *The first regular-season game ever played in the dome was a 23–14 loss to the New York Jets.*

The RCA Dome, located right in downtown Indianapolis.
INSET: A drawing of the future home of the Colts, which will open in 2009.

Dressed for Success

The Colts uniform is an NFL *classic*. It has barely changed in 50 years. The blue-and-white colors came from the Dallas Texans team colors. The horseshoe on the team's helmet—fans call it the "blue 'shoe"—was added in 1957. Before that, the Colts' helmet was solid blue with no design, or white with a single blue stripe.

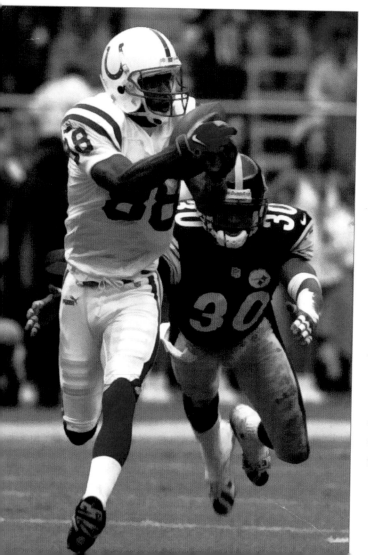

The team's jersey is blue with white stripes for home games, and white with blue stripes for road games. The number of stripes has changed over the years, but the look has been the same for many *decades*. The team wears blue socks with their white uniforms and white socks with their blue uniforms.

Marvin Harrison catches a pass against the Steelers. He is wearing the Colts' white road uniform.

The football uniform has three important parts—

- Helmet
- Jersey
- Pants

Helmets used to be made out of leather, and they did not have facemasks—ouch! Today, helmets are made of super-strong plastic. The uniform top, or jersey, is made of thick fabric. It fits snugly around a player so that tacklers cannot grab it and pull him down. The pants come down just over the knees.

There is a lot more to a football uniform than what you see on the outside. Air can be pumped inside the helmet to give it a snug, padded fit. The jersey covers shoulder pads, and sometimes a rib-protector called a "flak jacket." The pants include pads that protect the hips, thighs, *tailbone*, and knees.

Football teams have two sets of uniforms—one dark and one light. This makes it easier to tell two teams apart on the field. Almost all teams wear their dark uniforms at home, and their light ones on the road.

Peyton Manning looks for a receiver.
He is wearing the team's blue home uniform.

We Won!

The NFL owes a lot to the Colts. Their victory against the New York Giants in the 1958 championship game won over many football fans who preferred college football to the **professional** game. The Giants were the league's richest and most *glamorous* team. The Colts reminded fans of everyday working people. It was a great match-up—and a great game!

Johnny Unitas surprised the Giants by leading his team to two touchdowns in the first half. After 30 minutes, the Colts were ahead 14–3. The Giants came back to score two touchdowns in the second half, and led the game 17–14 with two minutes left. Unitas was "Mr. Cool" with the clock

Johnny Unitas and head coach Weeb Ewbank are all smiles after the Colts' first championship.

Alan Ameche scores the winning touchdown in the 1958 NFL Championship.

ticking down. He used **pinpoint passes** to bring the Colts close enough for Steve Myhra to kick a field goal to tie the game 17–17.

For the first time in NFL history, a game went into overtime. It was called "sudden death," because the game would end as soon as one team scored. The pressure was incredible. The Giants got the ball first, but the Colts stopped them. Once again, Unitas picked apart the New York defense. He moved the ball closer and closer to the Giants' goal line. Finally, Unitas handed the ball to Alan Ameche, who smashed into the end zone for six points and a 23–17 victory.

One year later, the Colts and Giants met again for the championship. The game was very close until the fourth quarter.

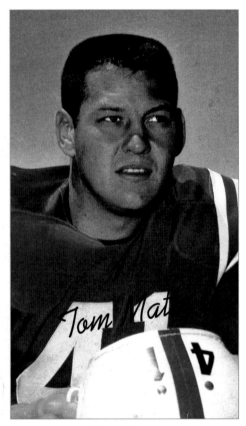

Tom Matte

Unitas took over again, and Baltimore won 31–16.

The Colts won their third NFL Championship in 1968. This time Unitas was injured. He cheered for his replacement, Earl Morrall, and running back Tom Matte, who scored three touchdowns. The Colts beat the Cleveland Browns 34–0.

The Colts won their fourth NFL Championship two years later when they beat the Dallas Cowboys 16–13 in Super Bowl V. It was a rough game that had many **fumbles** and **interceptions**. Some people called it the "Blooper Bowl," but it had a very exciting finish. Mike Curtis intercepted a Dallas pass with time running out, and Jim O'Brien booted a 32-yard field goal to win the game.

Kicker Jim O'Brien floats through the air after his
game-winning kick in Super Bowl V.

Go-To Guys

To be a true star in the NFL, you need more than fast feet and a big body. You have to be a "go-to guy"—someone the coach wants on the field at the end of a big game. Colts fans have had a lot to cheer about over the years, including these great stars...

THE PIONEERS

ART DONOVAN   Defensive Tackle

• BORN: 6/5/1925   • PLAYED FOR TEAM: 1953 TO 1961

Art Donovan was quick, strong, and a ferocious tackler. He also was a great comedian. His jokes kept the team laughing.

GINO MARCHETTI   Defensive End

• BORN: 1/2/1927

• PLAYED FOR TEAM: 1953 TO 1964 AND 1966

Gino Marchetti invented many of the pass-rushing moves you see today in NFL games. He often combined several moves on the same rush.

JOHNNY UNITAS   Quarterback

• BORN: 5/7/1933   • DIED: 9/11/2002   • PLAYED FOR TEAM: 1956 TO 1972

Many think Johnny Unitas was the best all-around quarterback in history. He had a strong and accurate arm, and played his best in the final minutes of close games.

RAYMOND BERRY   Receiver

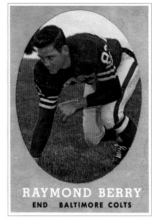

RAYMOND BERRY
END   BALTIMORE COLTS

- BORN: 2/27/1933   • PLAYED FOR TEAM: 1955 TO 1967

Raymond Berry was a great pass-catcher. He ran his **patterns** to perfection and almost never dropped a ball. Johnny Unitas could throw a ball to an empty spot on the field, confident that Berry would be there to catch it when it came down.

JIM PARKER   Offensive Lineman

- BORN: 4/3/1934   • DIED: 7/18/2005   • PLAYED FOR TEAM: 1957 TO 1967

Jim Parker was the NFL's best **blocker**. He was voted **All-Pro** as a tackle, and then All-Pro when he moved over to play guard.

LENNY MOORE   Running Back/Receiver

LENNY MOORE
BALTIMORE COLTS   HALFBACK

- BORN: 11/25/1933   • PLAYED FOR TEAM: 1956 TO 1967

For many years, Lenny Moore was the most dangerous player in the NFL. He was a super runner and a fast receiver—a man who could score at any time, on any play. In 1964, when everyone thought he was too old to play, Moore scored 20 touchdowns.

BUBBA SMITH   Defensive End

- BORN: 2/28/1945   • PLAYED FOR TEAM: 1967 TO 1971

When quarterbacks dropped back to pass, they kept one eye on their receiver and the other eye on Bubba Smith. He stood 6' 7" and weighed 270 pounds, and was one of the hardest tacklers in the NFL.

LEFT: Gino Marchetti **ABOVE**: Lenny Moore   **TOP**: Raymond Berry

MODERN STARS

BERT JONES   Quarterback

• BORN: 9/7/1951   • PLAYED FOR TEAM: 1973 TO 1981

Bert Jones grew up playing catch with an NFL receiver—his father, Dub Jones—so it only made sense he would become a pro quarterback. Jones was the team's best player during the 1970s. He was named the league's Player of the Year in 1976.

ERIC DICKERSON   Running Back

• BORN: 9/2/1960   • PLAYED FOR TEAM: 1987 TO 1991

The Colts like to "grow" their own stars, but in the case of Eric Dickerson, they were happy they did not. He came to the team in a trade on Halloween night in 1987, and helped them reach the **playoffs** a few months later. In 1988, the powerful runner led the NFL in **rushing** with 1,659 yards.

MARSHALL FAULK   Running Back

• BORN: 2/26/1973   • PLAYED FOR TEAM: 1994 TO 1998

Marshall Faulk was another "do-it-all" running back in the Colts' tradition. He gained 1,000 yards in four of his five seasons with Indianapolis, and caught almost 300 passes as a Colt.

MARVIN HARRISON   Receiver

• BORN: 8/25/1972   • FIRST SEASON WITH TEAM: 1996

Marvin Harrison was smaller than most NFL pass receivers when he joined the Colts, but no one put up larger numbers. In 2002, the fast and fearless All-Pro set a new record with 143 catches.

PEYTON MANNING   Quarterback

- BORN: 3/24/1976   • FIRST SEASON WITH TEAM: 1998

Peyton Manning's father, Archie, was a star quarterback in college and the NFL. By the time Manning joined the Colts, he already knew more about playing pro football than many of his Indianapolis teammates. In 2004, he broke the all-time record for touchdown passes in a season, with 49.

EDGERRIN JAMES   Running Back

- BORN: 8/1/1978   • FIRST SEASON WITH TEAM: 1999

Edgerrin James was one of the NFL's most feared runners from the first day he became a Colt. He had the strength to run right over tacklers, but he also had the moves to make them miss.

DWIGHT FREENEY
Defensive End

- BORN: 1/4/1978
- FIRST SEASON WITH TEAM: 2002

At just a shade over 6' 1", Dwight Freeney was short for a defensive end. But he put up big numbers from his very first year with the Colts. Freeney became one of the team's greatest pass rushers and tacklers.

LEFT: Marshall Faulk
RIGHT: Dwight Freeney

On the Sidelines

The Colts have had some of the NFL's best coaches over the years. When the team hired Weeb Ewbank in 1954, he told the fans that the Colts would win a championship in 1958. His prediction was exactly right. Ewbank had a good feeling for the mood of his players. When they needed discipline, he could be very tough. When they were playing well, he let them have fun.

Don Shula replaced Ewbank in 1963. He had played for Ewbank as a member of the Colts. He understood the team very well. Shula led Baltimore to Super Bowl III in January of 1969.

From 1975 to 1979, the Colts were coached by Ted Marchibroda. The team made it to the playoffs in each of his first three seasons. Marchibroda was on the sidelines again during the 1990s, after the Colts moved to Indianapolis. His 1995 team came within one touchdown of reaching the Super Bowl.

The Colts made it back to the AFC championship game after hiring Tony Dungy in 2002. He later became the first coach to win at least one game against all 32 NFL teams.

Peyton Manning and Tony Dungy discuss strategy during a timeout.

One Great Day

Every year since 1930, the Detroit Lions have hosted a Thanksgiving Day game. There is a lot of pressure to win on Thanksgiving. Millions of football fans plan their holiday meal around this game. No one wants to look bad in front of such a large audience. In 2004, the Colts came to town—and made the Lions look like turkeys.

Detroit decided the best way to beat the Colts was to have two men cover Marvin Harrison, the team's top receiver. When Peyton Manning saw this defense, he began throwing the ball to another receiver, Brandon Stokely. Manning's passes found Stokely in the end zone three times in a row.

The Lions had seen enough. They began to pay closer attention to Stokely. Manning told Harrison to go for the end zone. Three more times he threw touchdown passes—each one to Harrison. The Colts won the game 41–9. Manning's six touchdowns were one short of the record for a game.

Peyton Manning celebrates a touchdown pass.

Legend Has It

How did the fast-food chain called Gino's get its name?

LEGEND HAS IT that three members of the Colts decided to start a hamburger stand in Baltimore in 1957. A year later, they asked their teammate, Gino Marchetti, to join them. He was one of the most famous players in football, so they named the restaurant Gino's. After his playing days, Marchetti helped the business grow to more than 400 restaurants.

Gino Marchetti works the grill at his restaurant.

Who were the greatest pass-rushers in team history?

LEGEND HAS IT that the "**Sack** Pack" was. The Colts have had many players who could tackle the quarterback, including Gino Marchetti, Bubba Smith, and Dwight Freeney. But the team's 1975 defensive line (Fred Cook, John Dutton, Mike Barnes, and Joe Ehrmann) earned their nickname by setting a team record with 59 sacks.

Baltimore's famous "Sack Pack."

How did the Colts get their name?

LEGEND HAS IT that the NFL wanted Baltimore to have a team with a familiar name. In 1950, the league had a team in Baltimore called the Colts. This team went out of business after one season, but the fans liked the name. When Baltimore got another team in 1953, they simply took the old name.

It Really Happened

More than 50 years may have passed, but fans in Baltimore still talk about the afternoon of September 27, 1953. The Colts were playing their very first NFL game, against the Chicago Bears. No one knew what to expect. The team was made up of 'leftovers" from the old Dallas Texans, and everyone else on the field was new to the Colts—including their coach, Keith Molesworth.

The Colts played well in the first half, and the score was close. With just a few seconds left before halftime, and the ball on the 50

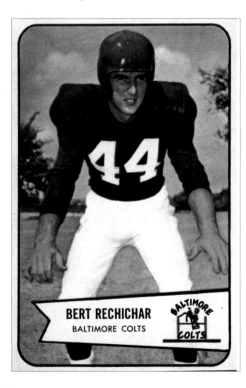

BERT RECHICHAR
BALTIMORE COLTS

yard line, Molesworth decided to try for a long field goal. Instead of calling for his regular kicker, Molesworth called the name of Bert Rechichar. The coach had noticed Rechichar showing off in practice, kicking balls more than 60 yards, and assumed that he had some experience as a kicker.

Rechichar ran on to the field. He was too scared to admit that he had never attempted a field goal before— from any distance. The ball was

snapped to the holder, who set it up, and Rechichar drove his left toe into the ball. Everyone in Memorial Stadium watched in wonder as Rechichar's kick sailed through the uprights, 56 yards away. Not only was his kick good, it was the longest field goal in NFL history!

Rechichar was not finished. In the second half, he intercepted a pass and ran it back for a touchdown. He also prevented a touchdown with a game-saving tackle. Later, Rechichar recovered a fumble to stop a Chicago **drive.** The Colts won the game 13–9, and Rechichar continued kicking and **punting** for the team for many years.

Team Spirit

The Colts have some of football's most loyal fans. When they played in Baltimore, they *sold out* Memorial Stadium 51 times in a row between 1964 and 1970. At that time, this was the longest "sellout streak" in NFL history.

Baltimore fans were shocked when the Colts moved to Indianapolis in 1984. Thousands continued to root for the team until Baltimore got a new NFL team, the Ravens, in 1996. When the people of Indianapolis learned that they were getting the Colts, they were overjoyed. They have supported their team in a number of creative ways.

The warm climate of the Colts' stadium makes it a good place to take children on cold winter Sundays. You will see more families in the stands than at most other NFL stadiums, and you will hear more young voices screaming when the team has the ball.

Colts fans have been known to do some
pretty strange things to show their love for the team!

Timeline

In this timeline, each Super Bowl is listed under the year it was played. Remember that the Super Bowl is held early in the year, and is actually part of the previous season. For example, Super Bowl XL was played on February 4 of 2006, but it was the championship of the 2005 NFL season.

1953
The Colts play their first NFL game.

1958
The Colts win the NFL Championship

1964
The Colts play for the NFL Championship, but are beaten 27–0 by the Cleveland Browns.

1955
Alan Ameche leads the NFL with 961 rushing yards.

1960
Johnny Unitas throws a touchdown pass in his 47th game in a row.

1969
The Colts lose to the New York Jets in Super Bowl III after winning the 1968 NFL Championship.

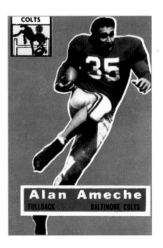

Alan Ameche

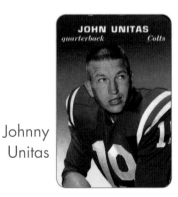

Johnny Unitas

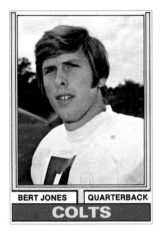

Bert Jones

Fans celebrate Peyton Manning's 49th touchdown.

1976
Quarterback Bert Jones is named the NFL's Player of the Year.

1987
The Colts trade for superstar Eric Dickerson.

2004
Peyton Manning throws for 49 touchdowns to set a new NFL record.

1971
The Colts beat the Dallas Cowboys 16–13 in Super Bowl V.

1984
The Colts move to Indianapolis.

2002
Marvin Harrison sets a new NFL record with 143 pass **receptions**.

Marvin Harrison

Fun Facts

INSTANT QUARTERBACK

In 1965, running back Tom Matte was asked to play quarterback in the last game of the season. All of the other Colts quarterbacks were injured. Matte wrote down the team's plays on his sleeve. He led the Colts to victory that day, and helped them get into the playoffs.

BIGGER IS BETTER

Art Donovan stood just over six feet tall and weighed 300 pounds. Everyone called him "Fatso" when he played, but Donovan got the last laugh. He was the first member of the Colts to make it to the Hall of Fame. Later, he made a lot of money writing a best-selling book. The title? *Fatso!*

YOUNG LOVE

Claude "Buddy" Young was the smallest man in football when he played for the Colts—just 5' 4". Before Young joined the team, Baltimore fans made fun of his size. As a member of the Colts, he was voted their most popular player.

WATCH THIS, DAD!

Two of the best quarterbacks in team history—Peyton Manning and Bert Jones—were the sons of NFL stars. Archie Manning played for three teams and threw 125 touchdown passes during the 1970s and 1980s. Dub Jones was a pass receiver who played in NFL Championship games for the Cleveland Browns in the 1960s.

MY TEAM FOR YOUR TEAM

The biggest "trade" in NFL history took place between the Baltimore Colts and Los Angeles Rams in 1972. Carroll Rosenbloom, the owner of the Colts, exchanged teams with Robert Irsay, the owner of the Rams. The players stayed in the same uniforms, but the owners switched offices.

UNHAPPY LANDING

In 1976, a small plane slammed into the upper deck at Baltimore's Memorial Stadium. The Colts and Steelers had just completed a playoff game. Had the plane crashed an hour earlier, the stands would have been full. Fortunately, no fans were injured and the pilot survived the accident.

LEFT: Buddy Young
RIGHT: The pilot survived this crash in 1976.

Talking Football

"It's cool to run over those smaller guys, but those big dudes—the guys who've been working in the weight room all week, just waiting for their chance to smack you—now I don't even try."

—Edgerrin James, on running away from tacklers instead of right at them

Johnny Unitas

"The thing I've found about pro football is that, no matter how good the defense is, you can always find a weakness somewhere…it's like a science experiment—you have to think every minute."

—Johnny Unitas, on his ability to throw touchdown passes

"I didn't call a play and think to myself, 'I wonder if this will work.' I knew it would work."

> —*Bert Jones, on playing with confidence*

"Always be yourself out there. Play your own game."

> —*Coach Ted Marchibroda, on the key to winning football games*

"When people stop and think about number 29, I want them to think of a winner, and a good person."

> —*Eric Dickerson, on how he would like to be remembered*

"I've never left the field saying, 'I could've done more to get ready,' and that gives me peace of mind."

> —*Peyton Manning, on preparing for each game*

"I'm a light eater. As soon as it's light, I start to eat."

> —*Art Donovan, on his football "diet"*

Art Donovan

For the Record

The great Colts teams and players have left their marks on the record books. These are the "best of the best"…

Johnny Unitas

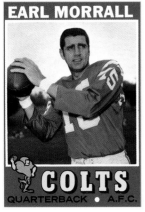

Earl Morrall

COLTS AWARD WINNERS

WINNER	AWARD	YEAR
Alan Ameche	Rookie of the Year*	1955
Lenny Moore	Rookie of the Year	1956
Johnny Unitas	Player of the Year	1957
Weeb Ewbank	Coach of the Year	1958
Johnny Unitas	Player of the Year	1964
Don Shula	Coach of the Year	1964
Johnny Unitas	Player of the Year	1967
Earl Morrall	Player of the Year	1968
Don Shula	Coach of the Year	1968
Ted Marchibroda	Coach of the Year	1975
Bert Jones	Player of the Year	1976
Marshall Faulk	Rookie of the Year	1994
Edgerrin James	Rookie of the Year	1999
Peyton Manning	Co-Player of the Year	2003
Peyton Manning	Player of the Year	2004

An award given to the league's best first-year player.

COLTS ACHIEVEMENTS

ACHIEVEMENT	YEAR
Western Conference Champions	1958
NFL Champions	1958
Western Conference Champions	1959
NFL Champions	1959
Western Conference Champions	1964
Coastal Division Champions	1968
NFL Champions	1968
AFC East Champions	1970
AFC Champions	1970
Super Bowl V Champions	1970*
AFC East Champions	1975
AFC East Champions	1976
AFC East Champions	1977
AFC East Champions	1987
AFC East Champions	1999
AFC South Champions	2003
AFC South Champions	2004

Super Bowls are played early the following year, but the game is counted as the championship of this season.

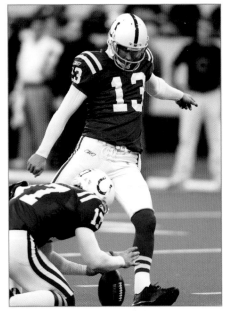

Kicker Mike Vanderjagt, a key to the team's division titles in 2003 and 2004.

Edgerrin James, the 1999 NFL Rookie of the Year.

Pinpoints

The history of a football team is made up of many smaller stories. These stories take place all over the map—not just in the city a team calls "home." Match the push-pins on these maps to the Team Facts and you will begin to see the story of the Colts unfold!

TEAM FACTS

1   Baltimore, Maryland—*The team played here from 1953 to 1983.*

2   Indianapolis, Indiana—*The team has played here since 1984.*

3   Bronx, New York—*Art Donovan was born here.*

4   Philadelphia, Pennsylvania—*Marvin Harrison was born here.*

5   Pittsburgh, Pennsylvania—*Johnny Unitas was born here.*

6   Smithers, West Virginia—*Gino Marchetti was born here.*

7   Jackson, Mississippi—*Tony Dungy was born here.*

8   Beaumont, Texas—*Bubba Smith was born here.*

9   New Orleans, Louisiana—*Peyton Manning was born here.*

10   Immokalee, Florida—*Edgerrin James was born here.*

11   Oakville, Ontario, Canada—*Mike Vanderjagt was born here*

12   Guatemala City, Guatemala—*Ted Hendricks was born here.*

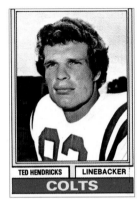

TED HENDRICKS	LINEBACKER
COLTS	

Hall of Fame
linebacker
Ted Hendricks.

Play Ball

Football is a sport played by two teams on a field that is 100 yards long. The game is divided into four 15-minute quarters. Each team must have 11 players on the field at all times. The group that has the ball is called the offense. The group trying to keep the offense from moving the ball forward is called the defense.

A football game is made up of a series of "plays." Each play starts and ends with a referee's signal. A play begins when the center snaps the ball between his legs to the quarterback. The quarterback then gives the ball to a teammate, throws (or "passes") the ball to a teammate, or runs with the ball himself. The job of the defense is to tackle the player with the ball or stop the quarterback's pass. A play ends when the ball (or player holding the ball) is "down." The offense must move the ball forward at least 10 yards every four downs. If it fails to do so, the other team is given the ball. If the offense has not made 10 yards after three downs—and does not want to risk losing the ball—it can kick (or "punt") the ball to make the other team start from its own end of the field.

At each end of a football field is a goal line, which divides the field from the end zone. A team must run or pass the ball over the goal line to score a touchdown, which counts for six points. After scoring a touchdown, a team can try a short kick for one "extra point," or try again to run or pass across the goal line for two points. Teams can score three points from anywhere on the field by kicking the ball between the goal posts. This is called a field goal.

The defense can score two points if it tackles a player while he is in his own end zone. This is called a safety. The defense can also score points by taking the ball away from the offense and crossing the opposite goal line for a touchdown. The team with the most points after 60 minutes is the winner.

Football may seem like a very hard game to understand, but the more you play and watch football, the more "little things" you are likely to notice. The next time you are at a game, look for these plays:

PLAY LIST

BLITZ—A play where the defense sends extra tacklers after the quarterback. If the quarterback sees a blitz coming, he passes the ball quickly. If he does not, he can end up on the bottom of a very big pile!

DRAW—A play where the offense pretends it will pass the ball, and then gives it to a running back. If the offense can "draw" the defense to the quarterback and his receivers, the running back should have lots of room to run.

FLY PATTERN—A play where a team's fastest receiver is told to "fly" past the defensive backs for a long pass. Many long touchdowns are scored on this play.

SQUIB KICK—A play where the ball is kicked a short distance on purpose. A squib kick is used when the team kicking off does not want the other team's fastest player to catch the ball and run with it.

SWEEP—A play where the ball-carrier follows a group of teammates moving sideways to "sweep" the defense out of the way. A good sweep gives the runner a chance to gain a lot of yards before he is tackled or forced out of bounds.

Glossary

FOOTBALL WORDS TO KNOW

ALL-AMERICAN FOOTBALL CONFERENCE (AAFC)—A professional league that existed from 1946 to 1949.

ALL-PRO—An honor given to the best players at their position at the end of each season.

AMERICAN FOOTBALL CONFERENCE (AFC)—One of two groups of teams that make up the National Football league. The winner of the AFC plays the winner of the National Football Conference (NFC) in the Super Bowl.

AMERICAN FOOTBALL LEAGUE (AFL)—The football league that began play in 1960, and later merged with the National Football League.

BLOCKER—A player who uses his body to protect the ball carrier.

DRAFTED—Chosen from a group of the best college players.

DRIVE—A series of plays that drives the defense back toward its own goal.

FIELD GOAL—A goal from the field, kicked over the crossbar and between the goal posts. A field goal is worth three points.

FUMBLE—A ball that is dropped by the player carrying it.

HUDDLE—The gathering of players where each new play is called.

INTERCEPTION—A pass caught by the defensive team.

NATIONAL FOOTBALL LEAGUE (NFL)—The league that started in 1920 and is still operating today.

NFL CHAMPIONSHIP—The game played each year to decide the winner of the league from 1933 to 1969.

OVERTIME—The period played to decide the winner of a game that is tied after 60 minutes.

PATTERN—The specific route a receiver follows on a pass play.

PINPOINT PASSES—Balls thrown with great accuracy.

PLAYOFFS—The games played after the regular season that determine who plays in the Super Bowl.

PROFESSIONAL—A person or team that plays a sport for money. College players are not paid, so they are considered "amateurs."

PUNTING—Kicking the ball back to the other team after failing to make a first down.

RECEPTIONS—Passes that are caught.

RUSHING—Running with the football.

SACK—Tackle the quarterback.

SNAPPED—"Hiked" the ball between the legs. The center snaps the ball into the quarterback's hands to start most plays.

SUPER BOWL—The championship game of football, played between the winner of the American Football Conference (AFC) and National Football Conference (NFC). The first four Super Bowls were played between the NFL champions and the AFL champions.

OTHER WORDS TO KNOW

ACCOMPLISH—To achieve or complete.

CLASSIC—Something that remains popular for a long time.

CONTENDER—A person or team good enough to compete for a prize or championship.

DECADES—Periods of 10 years.

FIBERGLASS—A building material made with fine threads of glass.

GLAMOROUS—Attractive and exciting.

SOLD OUT—No more tickets for sale.

SPACIOUS—Having a lot of space.

TEFLON-COATED—Covered with a slick, smooth surface of Teflon®, a material also used in non-stick cookwear.

TAILBONE—The bone that protects the base of the spine.

TENACIOUS—Unwilling to give up.

TRADITION—A belief or custom that is handed down from generation to generation.

Places to Go

ON THE ROAD

THE RCA DOME
100 South Capitol Avenue
Indianapolis, Indiana 46225
(317) 297-2658

THE PRO FOOTBALL HALL OF FAME
2121 George Halas Drive NW
Canton, Ohio 44708
(330) 456-8207

ON THE WEB

THE NATIONAL FOOTBALL LEAGUE   www.nfl.com
  • *Learn more about the National Football League*

THE INDIANAPOLIS COLTS   www.Colts.com
  • *Learn more about the Indianapolis Colts*

THE PRO FOOTBALL HALL OF FAME   www.profootballhof.com
  • *Learn more about football's greatest players*

ON THE BOOKSHELF

To learn more about the sport of football, look for these books at your library or bookstore:

  • Ingram, Scott. *A Football All-Pro*. Chicago, IL.: Heinemann Library, 2005.
  • Kennedy, Mike. *Football*. Danbury, CT.: Franklin Watts, 2003.
  • Suen, Anastasia. *The Story of Football*. New York, NY.: PowerKids Press, 2002.

Index

PAGE NUMBERS IN **BOLD** REFER TO ILLUSTRATIONS.

The Team

MARK STEWART has written more than 20 books on football, and over 100 sports books for kids. He grew up in New York City during the 1960s rooting for the Giants and Jets, and now takes his two daughters, Mariah and Rachel, to watch them play in their home state of New Jersey. Mark comes from a family of  writers. His grandfather was Sunday Editor of *The New York Times* and his mother was Articles Editor of *The Ladies Home Journal* and *McCall's*. Mark has profiled hundreds of athletes over the last 20 years. He has also written several books about New York and New Jersey. Mark is a graduate of Duke University, with a degree in history. He lives with his daughters and wife, Sarah, overlooking Sandy Hook, NJ.

JASON AIKENS is the Collections Curator at the Pro Football Hall of Fame. He is responsible for the preservation of the Pro Football Hall of Fame's collection of artifacts and memorabilia and obtaining new donations of memorabilia from current players and NFL teams. Jason has a Bachelor of Arts in History from Michigan State University and a Masters in History from Western Michigan University where he concentrated on sports history. Jason has been working for the Pro Football Hall of Fame  since 1997; before that he was an intern at the College Football Hall of Fame. Jason's family has roots in California and has been following the St. Louis Rams since their days in Los Angeles, California. He lives with his wife Cynthia in Canton, OH.